# Third-Class Relics*

*referring to articles that have come into contact with a first- or second-class relic

# *Third-Class Relics*

*Scott Dalgarno*

MoonPath Press

Copyright © 2025 Scott Dalgarno
All rights reserved.

No part of this publication may be reproduced, distributed, or transmitted in any form or by any means whatsoever without written permission from the publisher, except in the case of brief excerpts for critical reviews and articles. All inquiries should be addressed to MoonPath Press.

Poetry
ISBN 979-8-9899488-0-2

Cover Art: *Angel II*, oil on printed cotton, 8"x 10"
by Nathan Florence

Interior Drawings: Nathan Florence

Author Photo: Elaine Jarvic

Book design by Tonya Namura, using Fairplex Narrow OT

MoonPath Press, an imprint of Concrete Wolf Poetry Series,
is dedicated to publishing the finest poets
living in the U.S. Pacific Northwest.

MoonPath Press
c/o Concrete Wolf
PO Box 2220
Newport, OR 97365-0163

MoonPathPress@gmail.com

http://MoonPathPress.com

*for Astrid and Alyssa who hold tight
to their adoring granddad's ankles
and keep him from drifting upward*

*Contents*

**I**

| | |
|---|---|
| Angel Pauses | 5 |
| Winter Sunday in Portland with Franz | 6 |
| chopping a cypress | 7 |
| "My weariness amazes me" and it's only 6:00 a.m. | 9 |
| in the only tall grass left to mow, miguel ignacio naps after taking his lunch | 10 |
| Five Unmoorings and a Question | 11 |
| Question for Emily who was "called back" | 12 |

**II**

| | |
|---|---|
| "Marleen" Marlene, 1974 | 15 |
| Sacred Heart | 16 |
| In Van Nuys | 18 |
| Topography | 20 |
| The Raccoon: Once Considered Solitary | 21 |
| Old Man, New Leaf | 23 |
| Mea Culpa Mea | 25 |
| End-Stop Me | 27 |

**III**

| | |
|---|---|
| Madama Butterfly: 1930 | 31 |
| A Dream of Miles Davis | 32 |
| "Adiós Amor" | 33 |
| Diminishing Retorts | 34 |
| Meditation for those in custody or who long to be | 35 |
| Our Father | 36 |
| Pilgrim Visits Anchoress, Julian of Norwich, April 1410 | 37 |
| Small Pleasures | 38 |
| Lincoln Brigade | 39 |

**IV**

| | |
|---|---|
| Exquisite Corpse | 43 |
| Clark Kent Never Won a Pulitzer | 44 |
| Puberty in the '60s | 45 |
| The Afternoon You Drowned, Artie Flanagan | 46 |

| | |
|---|---|
| After-Math | 48 |
| Fate | 49 |
| Bypasses | 50 |

## V

| | |
|---|---|
| Divorce Flotsam | 53 |
| "…fool me twice…" | 54 |
| Blues | 55 |
| This One | 57 |
| Eyes Sewn Open | 58 |
| Letter to Our Adorable Zygote Who Went Unrealized | 60 |

## VI

| | |
|---|---|
| What if we signed up for this… | 63 |
| Secret kept from my grandchildren | 64 |
| Limbo | 65 |
| Caesura | 67 |
| Lunar Eclipse | 68 |
| Final Errand | 69 |
| Largo | 70 |
| Late Mercies | 71 |

## VII

| | |
|---|---|
| Perpendicular | 75 |
| Free Fall | 76 |
| Down a Hole | 78 |
| Falling Upward | 79 |
| Backwards Jesus | 80 |

| | |
|---|---|
| Acknowledgments | 83 |
| Gratitude | 85 |
| About the Author | 87 |

# Third-Class Relics

I

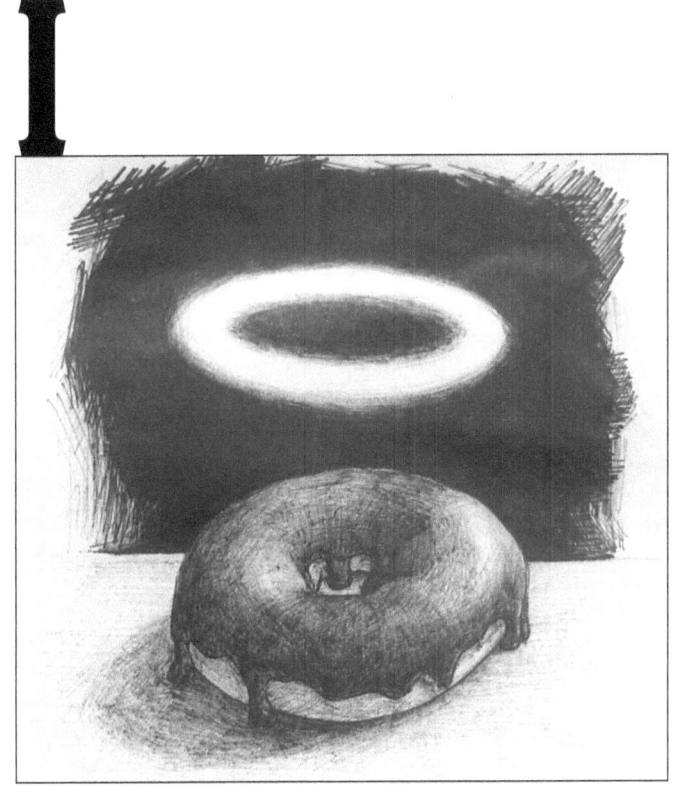

***Angel Pauses***
> *Girl Reading a Letter at an Open Window*
> Vermeer (c. 1657–1659)

Wanting to know what she knows,
he enters the painting. She stands
so still, so long, reading a letter
by borrowed light. It seems
she will read it forever.

     He hesitates,
the reflection of her hair gilding
the window brings to mind the virgin;
that and the angle of her head
above the paper, like the tilt of lilies
in conventional *annunciations*.

The air is pleasing, cool—
the curved lap of snow on the ledge,
an amnesty of white.

     He takes
his infinite time. He wants her
to overshadow him, overwhelm
him. He wants to carry
anything she might offer
for as long as it might take
him to deliver.

### *Winter Sunday in Portland with Franz*

Dreaming I'm the Virgin Mary, I wake in a sweat when Gabriel auditions me for a role in the nativity. Remembering that Giotto painted angels using sketches he'd made of sheep, I skip Mass and head to my favorite art supply store in the Pearl. Afterwards, I stroll over to Powell's where I hear my name on public address: "Kafka is waiting for you in the Rare Book Room." Famished, Franz and I split a Reuben at Kornblatt's. We discuss snowfall in the city; how one crow and his shadow equal two blackbirds. Passing on dessert, we Uber to vast Forest Park to glory in the winter canopy. The emerald damp elevates me. Kafka is a tall man—sitting, his fingers scrape the ground which, like branches of the avocado, begin to root themselves in the loamy soil. Like my sheltie resisting a pedicure, my friend withdraws his nails repeatedly, nibbling off the new tendrils. I do my best to pretend I don't see this. You'd expect it of Thoreau; maybe Rachel Carson or Anthony Bourdain, but Kafka? I ask after his fianceé. "Which one?" he asks. I tell him about my dream and the rude propositions angels are capable of. Franz nods, confessing that sex for him is just as disturbing; that he prefers to pay for it in cash instead of love. I feel like I might make an Oregonian of him until we grab espressos at Stumptown and Kafka sucks his through a cube of brown sugar.

### *chopping a cypress*
> "The cypresses still preoccupy me."
> Vincent van Gogh

Growing too close
to her sister cypress
I have chosen this one

(smaller by inches)
to sacrifice
so the other might thrive

I watch her still herself
each time I pause

like my own sister,
practiced
at gathering herself

shaken by her sons' aggressions
and a career that requires her
to be someone she is not

Vincent's impasto strokes
remind me
how the cypress is not
a solid but a liquid

mass    of     atoms
        more    space
than    matter

I aim my ax,
claim that empty wedge

open her      wider
        free her spirit
the way I wish I could free
      my gentle sis

Equivocations?
I know.

I am my ax

I wish to be the bird
    who flies
through her
    as if she were
mostly air

or paint her
with her mate
on canvas

where they can swirl
& flourish together

lit like Vincent's
sportive clouds

> *"My weariness amazes me" and it's only 6:00 a.m.*
> "Mr. Tambourine Man"
> Bob Dylan

There go the swallows
taking it out on the morning
drunk
like a foursome of lawyers

Their gripes filter
through visible cracks
in my reverie
conjuring an image—

        angels
climbing up
        cascading down
Jacob's aluminum ladder
    fist fights
erupting
        in the middle

When will the bloodshed end
        I mean
who at Agincourt knew
        he was fighting
the Hundred Years' War

Autocrats and autumn are making
mulch of the best part of summer

St. Cecilias turn to cider
on the Welsh low ground

and you, Dylan
Thomas
insist on remaining dead

***in the only tall grass left to mow, miguel ignacio naps after taking his lunch***

it's May and he's working ahead of the summer wildfires ahead of june bugs ahead of palm trees springing up in Alaska ahead of the next insurrection ahead of a mile-wide asteroid ahead of the Big One in California ahead of the little one his fiancée is expecting ahead of his first heart attack and the Second Coming ahead of Memorial Day which will be his last since on the next the woman he will never marry will come to the cemetery early with their baby in order to trim the grass around his marker with kitchen scissors, a shallow marker that will say he lived gently, left hardly a mark

*Five Unmoorings and a Question*

Pine lid drops;
widow takes an involuntary breath
followed by a sob.

Man in Buffalo
calls local police.
Please, he says. Please
make the wind stop.

Hooded parking meters—
a line of sinister monks.

Postage mocks you
with the word, FOREVER.

It's like I can't tell
if it's dawn or twilight anymore.

When your parents die
(I need to know)
whose daughter are you?

### *Question for Emily who was "called back"*
> *I must go in, the fog is rising.*
> Last words of Emily Dickinson

Home-stuck, sun-starved, your life
a scrap of stolen time in an upper room.
Were you shy or afraid you'd forget yourself

somewhere? Others found you
odd, volcanic, mad; a dessert
best served chilled. You survived

on hope's hollow calories;
purple plumes on a dying bird,
your worst trespass

house slippers caked with mud.
Naturally skeptic, you had no god
but Daddy—Mommy, his prophet.

You worshipped alone, breathless,
in the steepled church
of your own impending deathlessness.

# II

### *"Marleen" Marlene, 1974*
*...Mit dir, Lili Marleen...Mit dir, Lili Marleen.*

The "Summer of Love" is over; AIDS is yet to come. You're in the bar on top of the Mark Hopkins Hotel and fog surrounds Nob Hill the way white ermine crawls around Marlene Dietrich's shoulders. You're wearing a denim jacket from Goodwill. The maître d' doesn't like it but they're not busy and he lets you sit at the bar. They offer a hundred different martinis. You order a beer. It's her last set of a Thursday evening. All sequins, an oval of pink light accents her fur and face and leaves the rest of her to memory. Her whiskey tenor turns the place into a '20s cabaret. Forget about Liza—Marlene's the Blue Angel; she's the dish in the top hat in Morocco; all sex—no gender. You ask the pretty barmaid to deliver a note to her wrapped in a $5 bill. She does, and points you out. A lesser artist would think it an insult but this shimmering thing recognizes you. She's the USO and you're the soldier she's traveled to the front to entertain. Your note says, "Please sing Lili Marleen, but in German tonight." She looks at you. So remote; so available. She opens her mouth to sing. You're Gary Cooper for a minute. You're even Jean Gabin.

## Sacred Heart

I was slow awakening to so many things—
my mother's neurosis, the Soviet
threat, God's silence. In Miss Chastain's
fifth-grade classroom you said nothing,

just unhooked the oval charm from
your gosling neck and put it into my
hands. The look in your black eyes
made holes in me I have yet to fill.

Sitting on your porch under the large
plywood hand advertising your mother's
skill reading tarot and palms was all
I needed to know of bliss to keep a white

knuckled grip on breathing. Holding your
hand, watching as you tucked your tawny
feet up under the crimson fringe of your
skirt, I would have been content never

to rise again—but that summer you
moved. I only knew because a podiatrist
opened an office in your home—the hand
above the door replaced by a swinging

foot; your room become a doctor's surgery.
Word came today that poor Jesus likely died
of a blood clot breaking loose from his
mangled hands or feet—stopping his heart;

what long-haul air travelers may get if they
fail to stand and walk about. Pulmonary
embolism. Odd to think of Jesus dying
of something so pedestrian. So long

ago, and yet how palpable the memory of
my empty hand, your retreating feet, the ache
that makes my later catastrophes pale.

### In Van Nuys

I was raptured, temporarily, then recalled
due to a clerical error. There was the office-
generated apology, of course, with a Bcc
to God.

Des Moines looks so different to me now;
not nearly so plural. Apparently I wasn't
missed, but then, I've always been
the penguin in the red muffler.

I want you to notice me, but I still want you
to have to look. We're all of us faking it,
right? Only the young don't know that—
which makes them young. Everything shifts

over time. Now they're saying filthy
is the new dirty. Don't get me wrong,
I welcome the chance to come clean
about my hiccup with Jesus, but my people

have always adored their secrets, hording
the unstutterable, holding their cards
under the table. My grandmother was a Shaker
all her life. She had teeth made from old mah-

jongg tiles. Even her husband didn't know. What
must Jesus think of the news that all these years
he's been married. His wife, Mary of Magdala.
Hell, we don't even know what he looked like.

Maybe dark, short, with splayed feet and an eye
that wanders. *Christus Domesticus.* See them
commuting. "Pick a lane," he says, "any lane,
I don't care" (Mary likes to take her half out of

the middle). Afraid of being left behind,
she's forever offering to drive, while Jesus leans
into the tragic like some reckless geek magician.
Profiled in *People*, they're like rock stars

on holiday; see them walk, A-framed, purling
their way down Sepulveda, that Picasso body
of hers moving like a crab. He could fix that,
but likes her crooked, pink, & halting.

## Topography

I grew up with a scar on my cheek,
a perfect arrow aimed at my left eye.
My right is glass, so the arrow pointed
to the good one, as if to say, "Look here,

this window's open." Playing for change
on the street, I welcomed a touch
of the grotesque. Kids and dogs would stop
and stare, which made other people gape.

One of them had a neck like bamboo
with Japanese characters along her vertebrae.
She said my scar looked like Okinawa, in relief.

I'd take her fingers in mine and we'd close
our eyes and go there. The beaches were
wonderful, and, like sex, it was a cheap vacation.

When I stopped looking like a freak to her
she claimed she wanted a more practical life,
so I sold the Gibson and registered for night

classes. The week I spoke of marriage she moved in
with a one-legged biker we'd met at Burning Man.
I rebounded big, letting a surgeon make a playground

of my cheek, sanding it, like I was a sailboat
or a sake pot. Now I show up regularly in the pages
of *New Beauty*, but, yes, I confess I miss being huge
with first-graders and your stray Lab mix.

### *The Raccoon: Once Considered Solitary*

My mother keeps patting my head,
offering me her old marmalade cat
for company. I remind her that I'm fifty.
I tell her, "Grace, when you have
a raccoon you have everything;

looks like a cat, runs like a dog."
She worries because I'm on my own.
I remind her that she's single and full
of joy. She reminds me that I'm a man.
"It's different for you," she says,

and brings up Arnold, a dreamer
who can't tie his own shoes. She's been
his flashlight, his parachute, his 9-1-1.
Arnold's been trying for years to grow
squash with bar codes. "He's looking

to remove the middleman," she says.
"He's an idiot," I say. "A genius!"
she declares. "But you left him," I say,
reminding her she's better off without
him. When Arnold couldn't find a way

to remove "the middleman," Grace did.
Now that she's become her own best
friend she's angling to be Miss Alabama
Nursing Home, 2019. Hell,
I see her going to Nationals.

"Where is my ambition?" I groan.
I'm living with my brother. I know
a woman at Pet Center where I work
who's as lovely as a Mexican guitar,
but damn, she says being around

me just makes her want a German
Shepherd. I hear stirring below me
on the linoleum. My raccoon is looking
up at me, black eyes shining in the night,
a leash in her mouth. I remind her she is a raccoon.
She paws at the door.

## Old Man, New Leaf

I saw a pattern developing. I'd rolled over
my 401(k), two marriages, and that big-ass
yellow DeSoto I'd picked up in Oaxaca.

Deciding to rein myself in, I ordered oatmeal
with 2%. My God, I wrote
an ode. Motoring down, I began to see things—

Trout surfacing in the reservoir like wedges
of crystal. Mist descending feather-gentle
on lettuce at the Superette. I was
transported.

Hairs on my toothbrush stood
on end.

I made plans;
                ambitious ones.

I'd stack finger sandwiches, like cordwood,
house-high for the senior center.

I'd spread lakes of bark dust for them so pungent
in a summer afternoon you'd forget
orange was only a color. Done leaving

things to chance, I'd tie up every loose end.
No one again would say I was shiftless. Why,

if my daughter needed babysitting to go
to bunko, I'd be there for her—

we'd go halves on a sitter.

Change is good, I said. Change is our friend.

Made up my mind to finally, Yes! be buried
in that greasy coffee roaster—my hand
on the crank; my head set square in the sad

damn belly of the thing.

## *Mea Culpa Mea*

Here it is, only September first
and already it's as cold as yesterday's
gazpacho, and I'm wondering

was it something I said? The market
took a dive this morning. There was
no sign of it coming, so, being

conscientious, I decided to have
my white count checked. Okay, I know
I worry, but take Ukraine—there's no

end in sight, and I have reason to believe
(God will not be mocked!) it has everything
to do with that deduction I took this year

for my eye lift. Things in this world go south
so regularly, and inevitably it comes round
to being (I know) my fault. Sure, I could

have been a better husband, a way better
father. My own father said I had the kind
of brain to cure cancer, and here I sit,

considering how to assign blame for
all there is that disappoints. My mother
wrote to ask if I planned to call her

sometime, you know, before she died,
and it made me sad again for John Keats
and his poor Fanny and all the children

neither born to them nor neglected by his
obsession with art. Better dead at
twenty-five, I suppose, than leave a serpentine

trail of wreckage like Shelley, or Byron,
but I can't stop thinking about James Comey
who left that message on my iPhone asking

what to do about Hillary's emails and I was
just too lazy to call back. I know, I know,
it's true—I should be shot. I'd do it myself,

except who blames the victim anymore?

*End-Stop Me*

I spent the evening shopping for a new refrigerator.
It wasn't as much fun as it sounds.
A Chagall bride combed the aisles at Price Chopper.
Summer in Portland is one long costume ball and chain.
My dad believes one woman isn't enough and two are too many.
Don't boundaries mirror suggestions?
"Our marriage is hell, without the fires and the beatings," he says.
My poor mom.
St. Joan in a pointy bra and heels.
My family.
We're a people group with our own language, secrets, customs.
Any woman who smiles on me is a city of refuge.

I see lips as a patch of red tipping a blind man's cane.
What's off-limits to others is an HOV lane to me.

# III

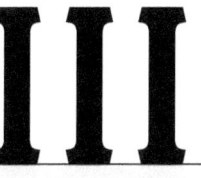

## *Madama Butterfly: 1930*

Outclassing the grape, vines of jasmine
circle the synagogue roof—a white crown
at Passover. Rabbi Yehuda raises his wiry
brows. "See," he says to his wife of twenty
years, "the Almighty is pleased." Un-
impressed, she feeds garlic bread
from the corner trattoria to her lawn
snails. Sorry she'd not done better
in the husband department, her father,
a renowned wunder-rabbi, shakes his hoary
head. Magda holds her own—training a parrot
to sing Puccini, her ancient poodle accompanies
on harmonium. Times are hard, few pay
any mind, but children love her, and Marc
Chagall comes round Wednesdays for opera,
sherry, and escargots.

### *A Dream of Miles Davis*
    (May 26, 1926 – September 28, 1991)

All at once the basement I grew up in is a hospital room. It's larger than that but there's all the familiar equipment and Miles is there wearing his shades, Miyake top, and plenty of bling. I remember rumors about him and AIDS so I'm not surprised by the long tube in his arm and the infuser that hums, beeps, and rolls with him. Miles drinks from a plastic bottle, coughs once, and plays a phrase from "Time After Time" which makes sense because I know he's dead. The phrases keep morphing like everything in this dream with Miles playing little bits of melody backward, or maybe inside out. Between numbers he's mute, like God; no patter. He makes quirky hand gestures to his bandmates, but the woman I'm with doesn't get it which disappoints me because she's gorgeous. Critics seldom get him, either, and I remember the Manhattan cop who bloodied Miles for insisting he was the headliner at Birdland, not some deadbeat hang-about. Hearing him again, I'm moved as much by what he leaves out of a tune as what he plays. He's bent over his horn in a posture of prayer and I notice the place is full of Hasidic Jews and I remember Sammy Davis Jr. converted so why not Miles? The tune is a call-and-response number. Miles is playing a prose line and his saxman, Kenny Garrett, echoes back in poetry and I see that my date is gone but I don't care. That's when my dad shows up like he did to take me home from the spring dance in 7th grade and I want to hide but it's my dad and he bought me my first six-string long before I knew the truly unique music of America came out of horns like Miles's and Louis's, not the hole in the belly of a Martin guitar.

*"Adiós Amor"*

Four Oaxacan workmen in orange kneel genuflecting over fresh mortar surrounding a stone step in a labyrinth in Ojai (palm trees hovering near like spirits of their dead relatives) half-listening to a battered boom box blaring *Adiós amor, yo fui de ti el amor de tu vida. Lo dijiste una vez, me lo hiciste creer,*\* their phones pinging as they chuckle over something a clueless gringo cannot, for the life of me, understand. I think of workmen in Pompeii millennia ago using the same materials to erect amphitheaters remembering the wrecks of their own failed affairs. Did the roots of the olive trees in Pompeii know the cataclysm waiting for them on that August day, AD 79, nourished as they were by rich volcanic soil, knowing the bargain we all make with earth and time and what is always coming and coming again from below? In the heat of our seismic passions rise the seeds of the demise of the loves we cherish today, plotlines performed in ancient Rome, Ventura County, whatever's streaming today; the dreams that haunt our every night peopled with our dead, our lying; the lovers we've yet to meet, magnify, misunderstand. God bless all the broken angels, all the fallen saints, all the misbegotten little gods we can't help but worship, curse, and worship again.

*\*Goodbye, love, I was the love of your life.*
*You said that once; you made me believe it.*
"Adiós Amor," Salvador Garza

### Diminishing Retorts

God said, "Who told you that you were naked?"

Descartes said, "Who told you that you were?"

Bogart said, "Who told you that, you . . . ?"

Monica said, "Who told you that?"

Dimmesdale said, "Who told *you*?"

Nixon said, "Who told?"

The ugly stepsister said, "Who?"

The snake said nothing.

*Meditation for those in custody or who long to be*

Mornings in April were short. We'd forgotten
to prune. Birds came back alone
or in 3s, pecked around, moved on

without nesting. Might earth
weary of fallings in love? Set adrift
those regrets,

bury your blushes; parade
your botches.
Entertain

the taboo. Blow
in your cellmate's ear.
Make a pass at the warden.

Where have manners ever gotten?
Eat. No . . . devour something. Appetite's
the thing. Hours later, praise satiety, praise

the impossible, praise the double-
bolted, your dead ends, overgrown,
moldy. Take the spoken word, "No,"

as your lover. Meditate on the Magdalene,
lonely, laying down her lithe shadow
before Jesus in his dreams.

### *Our Father*

prayed on his knees
prayed on his feet
during the ninth inning
of the seventh game
of the '62 World Series

prayed once in a foxhole
beside still waters
breeding mosquitos

prayed with tears running down
for his wife
for his ex-wife
in his sleep and dreams

prayed for his enemies
for his daughter in labor
before surgery
after making love
when he was beside himself
like a dying man
like his mother giving birth

prayed on the run
wished to pray without ceasing
like some ancient cloistered nun

## *Pilgrim Visits Anchoress, Julian of Norwich, April 1410*

Through a tight window, Julian
crouches over a bit of handwork.
Known for going nowhere
she has redefined the words *home*,
*here*, *prison*, *exile*. Your eye,
single, imagines her face. Her eye
never leaves her needle.
Unlike you, she knows where
she will die. She breathes, eats,
sleeps a seamless meditation.

Her chair is every chair,
her bed, every bed, her cell,
a wilderness, the first garden,
a temple of the spirit, the city
of God. She sets her face to go
nowhere.

Forever chaste, she greets you
like her own firstborn. Confesses
to you, as to a priest, that sometimes
shuffling about her tiny cell
she forgets where she is,
where she's going,
who she even is.

### Small Pleasures

> "This is beautiful country."
>
> John Brown commenting on the hills of Virginia riding to the gallows, sitting on his coffin.

My father sits outdoors enjoying an evening breeze off the Delta. I see only a red dot, the glow of his cigarette, and wonder if God was taking a cigarette break when a similar breeze wafted across Eden in the early days of creation. Dad's attention is on a portable shortwave—the marine channel; scratchy sounds of men talking to other men about depths, fish, tides. His aluminum chair rocks softly on concrete meant for a gazebo that will never be built. It would hide the stars. The man is happy, knowing how to savor the smallest pleasure. His wife will speak ill of this about him to anyone, will say that he never does anything large, seldom proposes anything more than a ride in the Dodge on a Sunday afternoon. I have met other men like him, men content with the lot of their cracker-barrel lives. I imagine they recognize one another by sight; men who want no more than a simple meal, an afternoon nap, a second cup of coffee; men who, if they were to be shot at dawn, would savor every puff of a final cigarette, the flash of the match, the soft light of first sun peeking one last time over ochre hills.

### Lincoln Brigade

> *"'Tis there that we wasted our manhood,*
> *and most of our old age as well."*
> "Jarama Valley," Woody Guthrie

Tucked between the two Great Wars
is the rotting cadaver
of a sad god

shot in the head
with the last tin bullet
of a lost cause

I who am skeptic
of righteous actions
write this

for my great uncle
lost at Jarama
who left behind a wife

and a fine bicycle—
more in love with death
and the ideals of liberty

and fraternity
than the plodding work
of a republic

I have only this casket
full of questions
for him and for you

my friend, eager
to save a world
so enamored with despair.

# IV

### *Exquisite Corpse*

> *Jesus came to Bethany, where Laz'arus was,*
> *whom Jesus had raised from the dead.*
> *There they made him a supper.*
> *John 12:1–2*

Four days dead and sipping soup, Lazarus
sits up, grunts, asks, "What's today?" He reeks
of tomb, but no one blanches at this banquet.

Sister Martha feeds him, wipes his chin, reminding him
of time and mass and the unforgiving weight of resuscitation.
There's that late-charge he thought he was clear of,

and the pruning, and that long look a barmaid
Once gave him, but that's all in Lazarus's moldy brain.
The guests merely gape; the vacuum of the tomb

has sucked every verb from the house, but Mary
has an idea. She produces a jar of nard, pure, priceless,
and gloppy as death. She smashes it like some Jeremiah,

peeling the fractured alabaster, lavishing the ooze
on Jesus's chapped knees and feet. All stand transfixed,
but Lazarus's eyes are still on Martha's spoon,

hovering a bit out of reach. Slowly he searches the room
for an explanation. There's Mary, as busy as a Martha,
and Martha, nonplussed, her heart churning envy and disgust.

What kind of household is this, Lazarus wonders,
where the dead are fed and the living embalmed?
Nothing sealed is safe; nothing at rest left undisturbed

by the merciless provocations of the living.

### *Clark Kent Never Won A Pulitzer*

"Leaping tall buildings at a single bound?" Rubbish. Superman's superpower is *not burying the lede*. He's a reporter for *The Daily Planet* but it's not a daily anymore, it's a weekly except for online, and the planet is dying. We're more primed for rescue than ever but who can help us? I hear the corpse of Charles Darwin (born the same day in 1809 as the corpse of Abe Lincoln) delivering a eulogy for the earth. Those who detest science & people of color hate them both. Can we fix this or are we all just petty functionaries assigning zip codes to random regions of our global Titanic? Lincoln's Gettysburg address was a national cemetery. I prefer Hawaii where names of fish are longer than the fish themselves. Captain Cook called them the Sandwich Islands, their in-betweens filled with sea salt & humpbacks. Ask Darwin why the whale's nose is on top of its head, he'll tell you, "That's where the air is." I look for answers in *Popular Science*: "Since the Big Bang the universe has been running away from itself with ever growing speed." Having trouble catching your breath? Here's some good news: "The dinosaurs aren't extinct at all. You'll find them alive and well in the whooping crane."

### *Puberty in the '60s*

The onset of acne; blonde girls obsessed
with Palominos; boys, often bottom-feeders.
One of them sits behind you in math, like a cat
napping on a birdcage.

The little courage you have you bought
with Green Stamps. Your mouth sports
an "appliance" that costs more than a refrigerator
and isn't much smaller. Mornings, you say,

are for other people. You like several girls
desperately. Everything you do
around them is like performing a lobotomy
on yourself.

You and your black-eyed cousin play pretend
lovers, holding hands, ramping up passion
to an almost-kiss, aborted repeatedly by giggles.
She asks if cousins can marry. You want to live

in such a world, but she longs for something
she's seen in black-n-white
between Brando and Eva Marie Saint.
Sex is a dirty word. Your parents are rattled

by the subject, but ask what you know.
This gives you power you'd gladly trade
for knowledge. Your mother worries
you are doing something she did at your age.

Your father worries that you are not. Wrestling
on the wet lawn, you and your cousin are struck
by summer lightning. Neither of you
is killed, but the sole of one of your Keds melts

into the shape of lips.

### *The Afternoon You Drowned, Artie Flanagan*

Beached, on your back, your eyes half open;
who were you trying to impress, jumping
from the tressel that way, Artie Flanagan?

I was between semesters, earning tuition
as a rookie fireman when our captain radioed
the ambulance en route, telling them to take
their time, you being, you know, dead;

we "summer help," standing there in the nonexistent
breeze, silent like you, having never seen
a corpse before—veteran firemen making jokes
about your too-small blue speedo and the fact that,
lying so low, you made no attempt to hold up your end
of the conversation.

Who knew that death could be that lonely?

I found your name later in the newspaper
below an ad for Pop-Tarts.

In my highly official,
               pre-Velcro
                            reflector-taped
                                            fire-retardant
uniform, I too was trying to impress
someone who barely knew I existed.

Your death stripped me naked.

You were hardly an Olympic diver, Artie Flanagan.
Like me, you were Martinelli's pretending
to be Dom Pérignon. I wasn't a lifesaver,
just a dimwitted undergrad who could comprehend
neither my father's infidelity nor his pleas
to reconcile.

What did I know about life's big questions—
all the answers, apt or bogus, waiting for me
along the far shore of my innocence;

my ride to them (time's checkered cab)
stopping for cigarettes,
in no hurry to pick me up.

### *After-Math*

At 12 you can't wait to be 17. There is one month
at 23 it takes you 6 years to get over. At 29 you want
to do college all over again. At 30 you ask time

to stop. At 40 you think you are home free
but Thanksgiving comes and with it, your parents.
Suddenly you are 15 all over again. Hormonal

changes at 50 give you the complexion you had
at 16. At 60 you have sex with a 35-year-old—you feel
very young and very old at the same time. Go walking

with them and people your own age refuse to look at you.
At your 50th class reunion everyone looks 20 years older.
You feel like 17 for an hour. When you see an argyle

pattern of lines in your neck you remember that you
first saw it on your grandfather. As your father is dying
you note that the back of your hands look just like his.

### *Fate*

> *He that is born to be drowned shall never be hanged.*
> Yiddish Proverb

It's our family's story—my great-
grandmother's recurring night-
mare: her youngest girl (a pistol)

drowning in the river. Frightened,
she moved the family inland. Soon
after, the girl slid off the roof

into a brimming rain barrel, upside
down. So, don't speak to me of
probabilities, 30% chance of showers,

50% mortality of marriage.
It's 100% or it's nothing. "I was this close
to leaving him," you say, but darling,

you stayed. I'm not interested in
the threat of a random asteroid,
and don't try to kid me

about Cleveland being "one out away"
from anything. We're, all of us,
whistling, like Bogart, in the noir,

which may explain why my father smoked
a cigarette called Pall Mall until the day
his own lungs filled up. He saw that flood

coming for miles but counted
on nicotine to keep his head
above the rising.

## *Bypasses*

I thought this to be a drop-off affair,
but when Reception asks her
for her living will, I decide to stay.
I cannot remember her name, this quiet,
duteous woman who I think of now

like the shy aunt you never quite got
to know. We wait in pre-op three hours
before the surgeon shows up,
and I take in the word, Mercy,
printed upside down on his head-wrap.

He repeats what she already knows—
that they cannot determine how many
bypasses she will require until they open her
chest and take a look. He says this
without using the words *open* or *chest*

and makes clear that he has little idea
what surgery might buy her. After a silence
that stings she lifts her eyes to ask
if she might have a heart transplant.
She is aware she is asking for something big—

maybe not the moon, but surely one of the moons
of Jupiter, it has so many. He blushes
with practiced apologies and in a moment
is gone. Any hope in the room bleeds out
and I see abandonment bead up on the glossy

white wall behind her. She reads this, I think,
in my eyes. Smiling crookedly, she says,
"I got heart-lucky once. He was sixteen.
Came in my bedroom window. Even sang to me.
I thought to make him shush, but I couldn't."

# V

*Divorce Flotsam*

Mommy
removes
a too-tight shoe

Daddy
can now
exhale

Making cautious
inquiries
over breakfast

little sister
and I find
it is transition day

again

Curled close all night
morning glories open
without a crease

*"...fool me twice..."*

My child tugs her kite
like a trout playing the breeze
connecting her to a fickle sky,
her manic attention reminding me
of the silver balloon that slipped
away; how she watched it out
of sight, like she watched her mother
at Gate A-35 on Momma's way
to a new life.

Tenants in our building come
and go like barn swallows
in summer. She has caught
the eye of a fresh one. Shy
like my girl, this one rings our door,
stands mute, then flees

in a panic. Always testing
whatever wiles or waters
she wades into, my daughter
trusts this "secret"
to but one of my ears.

*Blues*

That weekend at the beach
I woke wanting you,
your pillow cratered.
You'd risen

in the blue black,
meeting the morning barefoot.
Came back to the motel,
seaweed in your toes,

toting a turquoise float that had drifted
with infinite patience from Japan.
Salmon take years to swim
there and home—then spawning,

die soon after.
Such a climb back for you
after chemo
buying you purple

veins and little more.
I had suggested Venice—
romantic, exotic, a bucket-
list destination. "Disneyland

for the dying," you said.
Booked a motel
in Depot Bay instead.
Leaky faucet, tub

stained yellow,
constant rain; twin seagulls
hanging motionless
in the gale.

On our wedding day
my sister asked how
I knew you
were the one. I said it was simple—

your blues
were what I wanted
to be looking into
at my last.

*This One*

Death
grim but natural

a clock stopped
cold

Birth
the original riddle

What did my face look like
asked the Buddha

before my mother was born
And your face—

something in your eyes
looking at my mouth

recognizable
like a photo of you

I've carried in my core
since birth

or before
"Look for this one"

it says on the back
in pencil, faint

and small
the word, "Look"

smudged,
the Os, dotted

looking
like eyes

### Eyes Sewn Open
> *Stare... You are not here long.*
> Walker Evans

Childhood stare-downs. I exchanged looks
with classmates, goldfish, my dad's

Jeep Wrangler. In time they became tender—
the eyes of my newborn daughter,

the first hitchhiker I ever picked up
resembling my mother

in that snapshot from high school.
How vulnerable she was, nearly mute,

taking chances on the road, like my half-
sister who spent half her life (the middle part)

pulling green chain in a lumber mill; her laugh,
soft like water, having to prove again

and again she was tough as any man,
even some fresh from prison,

dissolving them with that long
look. I felt safe with my sister,

bereft without her. Some nights,
I lay awake in our house on the bay

watching searchlights
decorate the walls of San Quentin

plagued by waking dreams of men
skittering over those walls like banded

geckos, rowing stolen boats
toward my window,

unable to shut my eyes.

### *Letter to Our Adorable Zygote Who Went Unrealized*

I'm sure you'd have been a pistol.
You'd be eleven now, just beginning
to tell me you hate me. So bummed,
I never got to bounce you
on my knee.

I was already heels over head in love
with you
like you might have been
had you lived. We could have been
two shirts on one hanger.

Finally my life was NOT defined
by all my worst moments—
throwing up on that Ferris wheel,
telling your mother how beautiful
her sister was.

I'm such a failure. I mean,
even a lawn sprinkler
can make a rainbow.

Walking my despair
around the block here
the goddamn neighborhood
looks like hell: tipped garbage
bins, broken strollers, used condoms.

Your not being here
is everywhere.

# VI

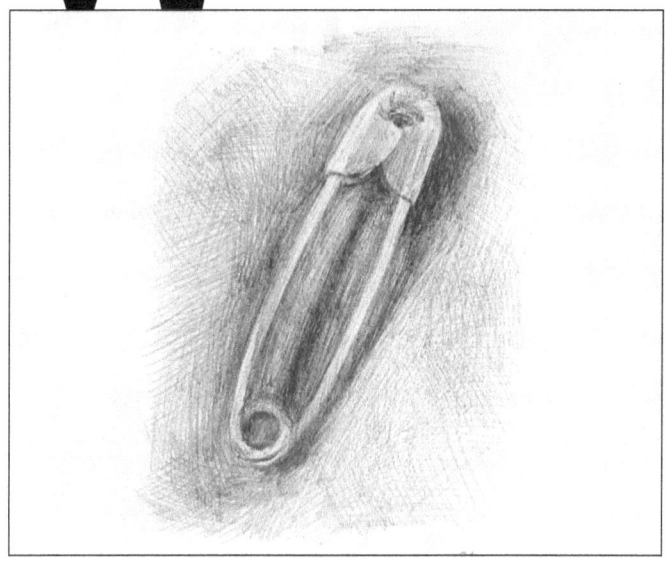

IV

*What if we signed up for this...*
> *27-year-old Mumbai man plans to sue his parents
> for giving birth to him without his consent.*
> BBC News, Feb. 12, 2019

...we're shown video, were offered maps of our lives *before* coming here. What if we said "Yes" to being vulnerable, knew well we'd be bludgeoned and bloodied, forgave our parents for their screwups before they bore us, beat us, blew their chance to be better dads than their dads were. What if we wrote it all off like moving expenses, alimony, our student loans. Would we feel less hijacked, more on board, less blindsided? Or would we still feel played, blame ourselves knowing beforehand what a mess we'd make of passion, portion control, parenting, and grandparenting, too.

### *Secret kept from my grandchildren*

Granddaughters tug my ankles
refusing me (their birthday balloon)
ascent,

have no idea how much of me
is up there already,
above, beyond

how many friends, family
I miss. The dead, damn them,
have taken so much—

tinsel on Christmas trees
tinny rattle of speakers at drive-in
movies, ten-cent ice cream cones

smell of mohair motoring home
               s p r a w l e d
across the backseat

Grandchildren won't know that world;
can't imagine this one
without me

Once, I pointed to a passenger plane
tiny
in the blue above

Three-year-old asked,
"What happens
to the big people"

Exactly

They get smaller and smaller
until they become
your whole world

*Limbo*

Left in a bed with hospital corners
& feeding tube, my life, a guttering candle;
Breathing, like pushing a grocery cart

from the wrong end. In the middle
of a dream about dying,
I die.

What gives?—
no tunnel, no bright light, no relatives
to greet me; just a scribble from my late ex

welcoming me to the first day
of the rest
of my death.

I find myself in the B side of Limbo,
the place Catholics used to send un-
baptized babies. It's true—

I've not been splashed
but I haven't
been shot, hung, drowned,

or crowned, either. Pope Francis says
there's no such place. What's become
of tomorrow; of yesterday?

Kettle never boils; dog circles
and circles but never lies down.
My derelict uncle shows up;

tries to sell me a watch
with no hands. I produce a wallet
with no money.

No matter. I'm busy,
assembling my own heaven
one pearly cloud at a time.

### *Caesura*
> *God hangs the earth upon nothing.*
> Job 26:7

When our arms were longer, the ground
higher up, we moved through the tundra
like Itzhak Perlman, without applause.

Once under the jungle canopy, abandon
describes our spiral way, slinging
compact bodies to heights where

they crest, nearly still—a moment,
surely, of joy. Not the banking turn,
nor the free fall demanding a choice

of bridge. No, a moment of phantom stasis
when things would come into view
you couldn't see as clearly at any other

place or time. Alan Shephard beholding
the crisp moon, his Mercury capsule
achieving apex; the violin's pause in Mozart's

G Major Concerto, holding Dudamel, the LA Philharmonic,
the Hollywood Bowl, an eighty-year-old usher
with plantar fasciitis in perilous thrall. Or my mother,

once the decree of her divorce came down,
gathered with her friends to "celebrate,"
before she woke up

the next morning,
asking, "What now?"

The moment after Frank Stanford
shot himself in the heart.
Before he shot himself

again.

### Lunar Eclipse

Now that he stands between us
your hair has become a corona.
Why have I not seen this before;

striking, and with highlights
I can't begin to describe? Little
things about you that once meant

nothing have suddenly captured me.
The way you park your tongue
on the edge of your mouth

when you steam our milk. The comic
effort you make to blunt a sneeze.
I find myself obsessing. It's so high

school. I know this will pass. Perhaps
he will move on and you will return
to being what you were to me

only weeks ago. Sad, that; sad
either way. Much of the time I am
blind. I get lost in the details, and then

I lose you, too. The cross-hatching
beside your eyes tells me we must not
be young anymore, but I feel the same

as always. Don't I? Most days I see
faces in clouds, but now there are days
when it's all clouds, no faces. Still,

this moment between phases has captured
me. Your hair, spectral; your air, a mystery,
now that he stands between us.

### *Final Errand*

Near the end they go
to Benares

a begging bowl
loincloth

enough money
in one pocket

to fuel
a funeral pyre

No need for earth
small call for air

just fire
then water

## *Largo*

There's your alto on your voicemail.
You're dead and sounding quite fine. Well,

everything overlaps. Everything bleeds
into everything else—physics and mathematics,

chemistry and biology, Bonnie and Clyde. What's life,
anyway, but a short stay in a quirky motel?

Still, they say it takes, on average, eight times
longer to accomplish anything than you expect.

I learned today that ullage is slang for the measure
of lack in a wine glass, and I think of you and me and all

we discovered together, and I let myself entertain
the thought, just for a moment, that we will never see

each other again. Oh, I know, even if we got
together now it would be different, you being,

you know, dead. That's the problem with grief.
Just when I'm sure it's passed, like you,

(go on, say it) forever,  here it comes
again, like Tony Perkins in drag, that old

Hitchcock staccato stabbing holes in the curtain
of my resignation, every bit as persistent

as this pulsing desire that prompts me
to keep punching your empty number.

## *Late Mercies*

Between Dead-Stop Coffee and your cancer scare
we dodge the rain ducking into your bungalow.
Your hair smells of lavender and heartbreak.
I smile trying to hide my fear of your history
but the care you take with small things disarms me:
thank-yous, second cousins, the single candle
by your bed. You unclasp your bra and I come un-
done. Unbuttoning my shirt you confess to thinking
you'd never have a lover again. Unwilling to be
as vulnerable I lean back and take you in. Your voice,
so vital, I fantasize the two of us together long ago
but you remind me that without our exes and grown
children we'd never have gotten lost in the same
place. You reach deep into me and pull out
a dark bird I didn't know was there. Your eyes dip
asking my permission to release it. I watch you
watch it out of sight.

# VII

## PRAYER CARD

Please remember in prayer today:

_____

Reason: _____

_____

_____

Request made by (Optional):

_____

○ Please **DO NOT** share with congregation

**NOTE:** Only the information above will be included in the prayer concerns. Share additional concerns on reverse side.

**9:00 Worship:** Please place on communion table during offering

**11:15 Worship:** Please pass cards to ushers at center aisle.

*Perpendicular*

Ancient Trappist monk, bent at the same angle
as his years, shuffles into chapel. In sight
of the altar, he bows even lower. Humbled are we
all; the universe, large; spring, profligate; our minds,
small; our years, numbered. Approaching sixty
from the wrong direction, I am still standing,
ambulatory. However, under radiation I lie flat,
frozen; bed moving under me, "gun" above,
stable, the sound of everything, clinical, opposite
of music. I close my eyes—a mortal meditation.
I'm a deer in radiological headlights. Where is God?
Above? Within? Everywhere? Nowhere? Motionless

I move on a thin sheet atop this swift round hospice,
counting all the beds I lie on before my end.

*Free Fall*

You are suddenly at the age
where friends become
dandelions. You blow
a kiss; they disappear.

Appalling.

You've known some
of them forever
but now their jaws
look like jaws
on ventriloquist
dummies. They don't
just sit down
anymore. No,
they let go and fall
into a chair.

It scares you.

You go to funerals
the way you used to go
to birthday parties.

You complain
that the ground
in cemeteries
is uneven. It's like
the dead want you
to fall on your face.

You lie down at night
and feel
the pleasant paralysis
of sleep come on

and wonder,
is this the trailer
for coming attractions?

You are a sunflower
bowing to autumn.

You are autumn bowing
to nothing at all.

### Down a Hole
*for Lucie Brock-Broido*

When I was very young every once in a while there'd be a black-n-white report on television of some child that had fallen down a well or who had gotten stuck in an impossible crevice somewhere deep in the earth and all day and half the night it would go on while regular programming would be interrupted and people would watch for a while and then go on about their business but their thoughts would be with the child way down in that hole as if it were their niece or their son or themselves—you'd be out at some public event or you'd be shopping and your mother would ask if anyone knew the latest on the child and we would all suddenly just for a day be one human family; then in the night sitting on the floor in your pajamas you'd be watching as the newspeople searched awkwardly for something new to say when finally the announcer's voice would rise and "Look!" said your sister pointing as someone would lift the child out dazed by the quartz lights trembling limp and thousands in the country would be bawling their 1950s heads off—even your father.

### Falling Upward

> *... he was carried up, and a cloud took him.*
> Acts 1:9

Gravity, they say, is all about mass. Big attracts,
big sucks, big pulls, big, like death, won't let go. Still,
we worship those who try: "Lucky Lindy," St. Michael
Jordan. Leonardo, bless him, forever plotting
how to fly or assuage the general jowliness of time.

Jesus was taken up, and Mary. St. Teresa of Ávila
had to cling to the rail during prayer to keep from floating
skyward—the Assumption being that things
sometimes fall up. But, come on, which way is up?
That is to say, which way *isn't*? If Teresa was a person

of such faith, why didn't she just let go? Like
the man I knew who, after being told he had "maybe six
months," immediately signed up for swimming lessons.
"Well," he said, "I just felt that if I could learn
how to float, I could learn how to die."

**Backwards Jesus**
> *The man who walks on his head sees the sky*
> *below as an abyss.*
> Paul Celan

Jesus descended from heaven feet-first. He got
a tearful welcome. Looking about for a place to nap
undisturbed, he entered a tomb. Angels promptly
walled him in. Three days later Roman soldiers

freed him, carrying him like a fishing boat to a place
called Golgotha where they hung him on a cross
by four neat little holes in his hands and feet. Later,
they accompanied him to a garden

where some men were napping. One of them greeted
him with a kiss. Indoors he performed for them
his first miracle, the joining of two halves of a loaf
into one. Word went out from Jerusalem when he set

up tables and chairs in Herod's temple. He charmed
a number of pigeons out of the sky into some very small
cages. From there he went out into the countryside
where he made a lot of people sick. *You have leprosy*,

he said to one. He touched another and the man's hand
withered away. One man, as sane as a judge, ran away
from him raving and throwing on his clothes. Then,
gathering a large crowd around him he mesmerized

them with stories of a young man driven off
by a horrid father against his brother's wishes,
of children dancing at funerals, and a tale
of the good Sadducee. He also preached to them

*Blessed are you who are full, for soon you will be hungry*
*Blessed are you who laugh, for you will weep*
*Blessed are you who are praised to high heaven for your*
*sinfulness, for yours is the kingdom of night*

When he was finished, his disciples went out
gathering food from everyone, about five thousand.
Later, three old men from far away came and took things
from him, but that was many years on when he was

very small, and soon would become only a sliver
of the purest light.

## Acknowledgments

I am grateful to the periodicals listed below for graciously publishing the following poems collected here.

*America*: "Exquisite Corpse"

*American Poetry Review*: "Backwards Jesus," "The Raccoon: Once Considered Solitary"

*The Antioch Review*: "Mea Culpa Mea"

*Bellevue Literary Review*: "Fate"

*Cagibi*: "Late Mercies."

*The Christian Century*: "Falling Upward," "Angel Pauses," "Pilgrim Visits Julian of Norwich, 1410"

*The Iowa Review*: "After-Math"

*NightWriter Review*: "in the only tall grass left to mow, miguel ignacio naps after lunch," "Letter to Our Adorable Zygote Who Went Unrealized," "Down a Hole"

Oregon Poetry Association: "Small Pleasures," awarded 2nd Place in the Prose Poem Competition

*Pilgrimage Magazine*: "Old Man, New Leaf," "Puberty in the '60s"

*Third Wednesday*: "Diminishing Retorts"

*The Yale Review*: "Largo" (published as "McGuffin"), "Topography" (published as "TMI"), "Sacred Heart," "Bypasses," "In Van Nuys" (published as "Jesus Turns Up in Van Nuys, but his Number is Still Unlisted"), "Caesura"

*Gratitude*

I am grateful to Dr. Paul Mariani who first expressed interest in my poems and gave me the encouragement I needed to explore new manners of expression.

I am also so fortunate to have benefited from the kindness of Sandy McClatchy who welcomed my poems to *The Yale Review* for ten years.

Finally, I want to express my deep appreciation to four poets who have been my first readers over many years—Dee Casalaina, Lisa Gustavson, Katherine January, and Kim Welliver. They have made this a much better book.

## *About the Author*

Scott Dalgarno finds abundant inspiration from the mystic, Julian of Norwich, the poet, Elizabeth Bishop, the artistry of Jon Batiste, and several coastal redwoods in the Bolling Grove.

While he writes a lot of prose, he finds that writing poetry can be an out-of-body experience, occasionally transporting him to a zone where time does not exist and is not age-bound.

He lives among firs and dogwoods in Lake Oswego, Oregon, where he works for issues of justice. *Third-Class Relics* was a finalist for the 2024 Sally Albiso Prize. It is his first collection of poems.

Scott Dalgarno's website can be found at www.ScottDalgarno.org.

www.ingramcontent.com/pod-product-compliance
Lightning Source LLC
LaVergne TN
LVHW041622070526
838199LV00052B/3214